Legal Reference Library
Volume III

by

John Philip Mason

While we have done our best to give you useful and accurate information in this book, the publisher and the author do not accept responsibility for any interpretation or application by the reader of this book. Laws change frequently and are subject to different interpretations. If you want legal advice backed by a guarantee, you should hire an attorney. This book is not a substitute for an attorney, and it does not attempt to answer all questions about every situation you may encounter. The publisher and author urge the reader to consult an attorney for appropriate advice on specific legal situations as circumstances dictate.

SANTA MONICA PRESS
P.O. Box 1076
Santa Monica, CA 90406-1076
Printed in the United States

Introduction

Do you know what legalese is? Legalese is the technical jargon used by lawyers; you know, those words that seem to go on forever, that seem as if they were designed for the sole purpose of preventing people like you and me from understanding them! Examples of legalese include: boilerplate, caveat, voir dire, and usury. Just looking at words like these probably makes you wish that you had studied harder in high school English class!

Well, there is one thing that you can rest assured about: you are not alone in your inability to comprehend the language of the law. That's why this book has been written. It is intended to serve as a useful reference guide from which you can cull the definitions to any common legal terms that you do not understand. In other words, this book will help you translate legalese into every day language.

Before I go any further into this introduction, I want to make sure that you understand that the definitions provided in this volume have all been simplified. They simply enable you to get the basics of legal terminology, without necessarily familiarizing you with every subtle nuance and detail. As such, this book is by no means meant as a substitute for a competent attorney. Should you ever need to draft a contract, for example, don't think that this book will help you generate a correct and legal document. Rather, it will allow you to understand the meaning of a document that has been written by a trained legal professional.

When will you have the opportunity to use this book?

For starters, if you're reading this volume of the *Legal Reference Library*, then you've probably already leafed through at least a few pages of the first two volumes. The first two volumes are a handy and concise summary of many major fields of law, including such topics as the legal concerns associated with buying a house, driving a car, paying your taxes, and even owning a swimming pool. For the most part, the first two volumes were written in everyday English (if they weren't, then they wouldn't be all that handy!). And whenever legal terms were used, I attempted to include concise definitions of those words. However, this volume contains slightly more detailed definitions, which will better enable you to understand the meanings of those terms. *So, the first reason that you have for using this volume is to help clarify any difficult passages in the first two volumes of the* Legal Reference Library.

But is that all this book is useful for?

Of course not!

Regrettably, America is becoming more and more litigious everyday. That means that the number of law suits is on the rise. Therefore, the chances of your being involved in some sort of a legal battle is higher than ever before. As such, you should arm yourself with the basic knowledge that you need in order to understand the workings of the American legal system. If you are ever entangled in a legal dispute, for example, will you know the ramifications of trying to resolve that dispute through arbitration rather than in a court of law? This book will define the difference between these two forums for you. *So the second reason that you have for using this book is to help you understand the terminology used in legal proceedings.*

As America is becoming more litigious than ever before, people are now doing everything in their power to prevent the kind of misunderstandings that lead to legal disputes. As such, people are signing contracts for just about any agreement they make. You will have to sign a contract if you buy a house, accept a credit card, or even allow your children to participate in sporting activities at school. Don't you think it is important to understand the meaning of the contracts that you sign? *So the third reason for using this book is to help you understand the language that goes into contracts and other agreements that are designed to avert legal battles.*

Finally, I'm not sure if you've noticed it, but the frequency with which legal terminology is popping up in the media is quite disconcerting. It seems to me that whenever I see a commercial for a product on TV, or read a printed ad for that product, there is always some kind of "fine print" that goes along with it. For example, if you've ever seen a television commercial advertising special incentives for buying a new car, then you might have noticed a paragraph of really small text written at the bottom of the screen, as well as a narrator very quickly reading a list of the terms and conditions under which these incentives are offered. Other examples of this fine print can be seen on the entry blanks to contests and sweepstakes. If you're anything like me, then you're sick of reading phrases like "Void where prohibited." *So the final reason that you have for using this book is to help you understand the fine print that accompanies just about every advertisement or offer you will see for the rest of your life!*

Not a bad list of reasons for having a small book like this on hand, is it?

Now that you know *why* you should use this book, *how* should you go about using it?

This book is very simple to use. It is set up like a normal dictionary. That is, all of the words contained on these pages are listed in alphabetical order, and they are followed by their definitions. Therefore, if you want to know the meaning of a word, then you should simply leaf through the pages until you find that word. For example, if you know someone who passed away recently, then you might have heard the word "Administrator." But what exactly does this word mean? The definition of administrator can be found on page 17, and it is presented in the following format:

Administrator: The person appointed by a court of law to handle all matters relating to a decedent's estate, if the decedent passed away without leaving a will.

But wait a second! What exactly do the words "decedent" and "will" mean?

As legal terms tend to be rather complex, sometimes their definitions might even contain words with which you are unfamiliar, as in the above example. But do not worry, because these unfamiliar words are also defined within this book! So, if you were trying to find the meaning of the word "administrator," you would then have to look up two additional words: "decedent" (found on page 34) and "will" (found on page 117). Their definitions are as follows:

Decedent: Someone who is dead.

Will: The written record of how a decedent wants his or her estate divided up.

So, by combining these definitions you can come to understand that "administrator" means the following:

"The person appointed by a court of law to handle all matters relating to a decedent's (someone who is dead) estate, if the decedent passed away without leaving a will (written record of how he or she wants his or her estate divided up)."

You now have a simple and straightforward definition for a complex legal term!

As you can see from the above example, legal terminology is not that difficult to decipher, but it is difficult to know when a certain term is appropriate. That is why I indicated earlier that this book should be used to help you understand any complex terms, but it should not be used in the place of a competent lawyer.

I would like to end this introduction by indicating that I have left a few pages blank at the end of this volume. I believe that a practical research guide, such as this, should be as easy to use as possible. And I believe that one aspect of ease of use is a section for you to jot down notes. Suppose you are interested in looking up several words simultaneously; I want you to have a place where you can write down all of those words. Then you can flip through the book until you find the appropriate page numbers for each of the words, and you can write these page numbers down. Then you will be organized and prepared in such a way that you won't accidentally forget one of the words.

Now that you have had the chance to read this brief introduction, there is no further need for delay. Simply turn the page until you find the word for which you are looking, and the rest is up to you!

A

A.A.A.: American Arbitration Association.

A.A.L.S.: Association of American Law Schools.

A.B.A.: American Bar Association.

Abandon: To give up the right to something.

Abduct: To take someone against their will.

Abjure: To relinquish a certain right or privilege.

Abridge: To edit, censor, or lessen.

Abrogate: To take back or rescind.

Abscond: To go into hiding unlawfully.

Absolve: To remove the blame from someone.

Abstract of Title: A brief summary outlining who owns a piece of real estate or property.

Accessory: Someone who helps another perpetrate a crime without actually being at the scene of the crime.

Accomplice: Someone who helps another perpetrate a crime at the scene of the crime.

Accord: An agreement where one person accepts less than what he was originally owed.

Accuse: To charge someone with a crime.

A.C.L.U.: American Civil Liberties Union

Acquit: To free someone from an accusation.

Act of God: An occurrence, such as a flood, which is beyond reasonable human control.

Action: A trial or other legal proceeding.

Addendum: An addition to a document.

Adjure: To promise or swear.

Administrator: The person appointed by a court of law to handle all matters relating to a decedent's estate, if the decedent passed away without leaving a will.

Admit: To indicate that something is true or correct.

Admonish: To punish or warn someone sternly.

Adopt: To invite a child to live with you as if he or she were your own natural child, and to bear all of the rights and responsibilities of parenting that child.

Affidavit: A written testimony that is signed in the presence of a notary public.

Age of Consent: The age when someone can legally get married.

Age of Majority: The age when someone is legally no longer considered a minor.

Aggravated Assault: An attack on someone which is so violent that the person could die.

Agreement: Essentially a contract, but it is often thought of as less "serious."

A.K.A.: Also known as.

Alias: A second name for someone.

Alibi: A crime suspect's excuse, indicating that he could not have been the perpetrator of the crime.

Alien: A citizen of a foreign country.

Alimony: Payments made to one's ex-spouse following the break-up of a marriage.

Amendment: An alteration to an already existing document.

Amnesty: A promise that someone will not be punished, even if they committed a crime.

Annulment: The complete dissolution of a marriage.

Appeal: To attempt to overturn the decision of a court of law.

Appellant: The person who makes an appeal.

Appropriate: To take an item.

Arbiter: A person who attempts to settle a disagreement as impartially as possible.

Arbitration: Similar to a court proceeding, but generally less expensive, a method for settling disputes with impartiality. Arbitration has all the same legal status as a case that is argued in court, and it is usually overseen by a retired judge. Both sides in a dispute must agree to arbitration instead of taking their claim to court.

Arbitrator: The impartial overseer of arbitration. Usually a retired judge.

Arrest: When the police take a suspect into custody.

Arson: Setting a building on fire.

Artificial Person: An entity that, for the purposes of the law, is treated like an individual. A company is an example of an artificial person.

Assault: An attack made on someone.

Associate: An attorney who practices law as part of a large firm.

Assurance: Insurance or promise.

Attempt: To try to do something.

Attest: To swear to the truth of a statement.

Attorney: A lawyer.

Attorney of Counsel: A secondary lawyer

who helps a main lawyer argue a case in court.

Attorney of Record: The main lawyer in a legal action.

Attorney-Client Privilege: The right of an attorney and his client to keep their communications and correspondence private.

Audit: A review of someone's financial records.

B

Bad Faith: Dishonesty when conducting business.

Bail: Money paid to the court enabling a criminal suspect to leave prison until the time of his trial. The bail is usually quite expensive, as it acts as insurance that the suspect will return at the time of his trial. The bail money is returned if the suspect shows up, but it is kept if he does not.

Bankrupt: To be broke in the eyes of the government. If one is officially bankrupt, then certain debts no longer have to be paid at the assigned time.

Bar Exam: The exam that a lawyer must take in order to practice the law in a specific state.

Barter: To trade items that have value but are not money.

Bastard: A child whose parents were not married.

Batter: To beat someone.

Bequeath: To leave an item to someone in a will.

Bequest: The item that is bequeathed.

Betroth: Engage to be married.

Beyond Reasonable Doubt: More likely than not. If you are ever on a criminal jury, you will be told not to vote guilty unless you believe that the suspect was guilty "beyond a reasonable doubt."

Bigamy: To be married to more than one person at a time.

Bill: An invoice indicating that payment is due.

Bill of Rights: The first ten amendments to the American Constitution.

Bill of Sale: A receipt.

Bind: To require.

Blackmail: To threaten to reveal a secret about someone if that person does not pay money.

Boilerplate: Legal jargon that does not affect a particular document.

Bona Fide: True.

Boycott: To refuse to do business with someone in hopes of changing a business practice.

Breach of Contract: Not meeting the requirements set forth in a contract.

Breaking and Entering: To enter a building without permission, usually with the intention of committing burglary.

Breathalyzer: A test administered by the police to see if someone is drunk.

Brief: A legal document.

Burglary: To steal any items within a dwelling or building.

Bylaws: The rules established by a company or organization to insure against mismanagement.

C

Capital: Any asset that can be used to generate income. For example, if one invests $5,000 into starting a business in order to earn a living, then the $5,000 is capital.

Capital Offense: A crime for which the punishment may be death.

Capital Punishment: To punish someone by putting them to death.

Caption: The title of a court document.

Case: A matter that is being tried in court.

Cash: Money.

Casualty: Loss, damage, or injury.

Cause: A reason to do something.

Caveat: A warning.

Censor: To edit the content of a piece of information in order to remove anything offensive.

Censure: To scold or reprimand.

Chapter 11: A type of bankruptcy faced by businesses.

Character Witness: Someone who attests to the character or reputation of someone else. For example, someone who has a priest as a character witness might seem less likely to have committed a crime in the eyes of the court.

Charge: To accuse someone of committing a crime.

Child Abuse: To harm a child either physically or emotionally.

Child Support: A payment made by one parent to another after the break-up of a marriage in order to assist with the costs of raising a child.

Choate: Complete.

Circumstantial Evidence: Indirect evidence that is not based on direct knowledge.

Citizen: A legal member of a country.

Civil: Private. Not criminal.

Civil Law: Laws pertaining to one's private rights, as opposed to criminal laws.

Civil Rights: Rights granted to all peoples by the American Constitution, regardless of race, gender, or religious affiliation.

Claim: To assert a right.

Class Action: A legal case that is started by many people. Usually, only one or two of those people are present in court, as representatives of all the rest.

Clause: An individual section or point in a contract or agreement.

Closed Court: A court trial where the general public is not allowed to attend and watch the proceedings.

Closed Shop: A business where the employees are required to become members of a union.

Closing: The final step in a deal.

Closing Statement: An attorney's final words to a jury regarding a court case.

Codicil: An addendum to a will.

Cohabitate: To live together.

Collateral: An item that is promised to a lender if the borrower fails to make payments. For example, when you buy a home, you get a mortgage, or home loan, from a bank. The bank is the lender, you are the borrower, and the house itself is collateral. If you fail to make mortgage payments, therefore, the bank has the right to take your house away.

Collusion: Working together in order to harm someone else.

Commercial Paper: A promissory note, or I.O.U.

Commodity: Personal belonging.

Common Law Marriage: When a couple has lived together for long enough that their relationship is essentially a marriage, even though they are technically not married.

Commute: To lessen a punishment.

Competent: Being of sound mind and body. For example, if you can prove that someone was insane when they wrote a will, then they were *incompetent*, and their will is nullified.

Complainant: See plaintiff.

Complaint: The document which initiates a legal action, clearly setting forth all of the damages that the plaintiff claims were caused by the defendant.

Condemn: To declare a building unsafe.

Conformed Copy: A duplicate copy of a legal document that has been filed with a court of law. The conformed copy is stamped by the court, and it is your proof that the document was filed.

Consanguinity: A family relationship.

Consent: To agree or yield.

Consequential Damages: Indirect damages from an incident. For example, if you get involved in a fender bender, then the direct damage is the damage to your car. An indirect damage might be your inability to travel to work until the car is fixed.

Consignment: The sale of goods through a third party. For example, if you ask your brother to sell your car for you, then he is selling it for you on consignment.

Conspire: To work in a group in order to break the law.

Construe: To interpret the meaning. For example, some laws are quite vague, and it is up to a judge to construe their meanings.

Contingency: To pay an attorney if he wins your case.

Contraband: Illegal goods. For example, Cuban cigars are contraband in America.

Contract: An agreement between several people.

Controlled Substance: A drug that is either illegal or requires a special prescription from a doctor.

Convict: To find someone guilty of a crime.

Copyright: The right to sell or profit from a piece of information. For example, the author of a book usually owns the copyright, which means that other people cannot use any portions of it without his permission.

Corporal Punishment: Physical, but not lethal, punishment for a crime. Flogging is a notable example.

Correctional Facility: A jail.

Costs: In the legal arena, any costs associated with an action that do not include the lawyer's fee. For example, if documents must be photocopied, then there are costs associated with such a service.

Cotenancy: When several people reside in one dwelling.

Counsel: A lawyer.

Counterfeit: Bogus or false.

Court: A place where disputes are settled officially by an impartial judge.

Covenant: An agreement.

Crime: An act that is a violation of the law.

Criminal: A convict.

Criminal Law: Laws concerning crimes, as opposed to civil law.

Cross-Examination: When a lawyer asks a witness questions in court, that is known as examination. The lawyers for both the defendant and the plaintiff bring witnesses to court. When a lawyer questions his own witness, that is referred to as direct-examination. When a lawyer questions the opposing party's witness, that is called cross-examination. The point of cross-examination is to destroy the credibility of a witness.

Culpable: Guilty.

Curfew: A time after which one is not allowed to be out on the streets.

Custody: To exert control over something, usually a person. For example, after the break-up of a marriage, the court must decide which parent gets custody of the children. That parent will keep the children in his or her home.

D

D.A.: District Attorney.

Damages: A form of compensation that is given to someone in order to make up for a loss or tragedy.

Deadlock: The state a jury is in when it can not reach a verdict.

Deadly Force: A force so violent that it will most likely result in the death of another person.

Debt: An obligation to make payment. An amount that is owed.

Debtor: Someone with a debt.

Decedent: Someone who is dead.

Deceit: Deliberate lie.

Declaration: A statement that recounts the facts of an incident. It differs from an affidavit in that it is not sworn to in the presence of a notary public.

Dedication: The act of giving a privately owned piece of land to the public.

Deed: A written document indicating the ownership status of a piece of land or real estate.

Defamation: Harming the reputation or stature of an individual by denouncing their character.

Default: Not living up to a duty. For example, if you do not pay your mortgage on time each month, then you are in default of your mortgage payments.

Defendant: The person or persons in a legal action who are accused of causing harm to the plaintiff. The burden to prove that such harm was actually caused always rests on the plaintiff.

Defense: The excuses made by a defendant in order to demonstrate that the plaintiff was not actually harmed by the defendant.

Defer: To put off temporarily or delay.

Delegate: A person appointed to fulfill the responsibilities of someone else.

Demur: If a defendant demurs, he is trying to indicate that he does not feel that any damages were caused to the plaintiff whatsoever, let alone any damages specifically caused by the defendant.

Deny: To claim that something is not true.

Dependent: A person who relies on the financial support of others (usually children).

Deposition: A question-and-answer session between an attorney and a witness that is performed under oath. If the witness lies, then he is guilty of perjury.

Depreciate: To lose value. For example, the value of a house tends to depreciate if the crime rate goes up in the neighborhood where the house is located.

Detain: To arrest.

Direct-examination: See cross-examination.

Disbar: To forbid a lawyer to practice the law. This occurs if the lawyer is found to have broken the law or harmed his client.

Disclaimer: A warning indicating that a certain party is not responsible for the outcome of an event.

Discovery: The attempt to learn more about an opponent in a legal action by taking depositions, asking for permission to view documents possessed by the opponent, and asking the opponent to submit written answers to a series of questions.

Disenfranchise: To remove all of the rights of citizenship from a citizen.

Disorderly Conduct: To act in an unacceptable manner in public, such as being boisterously drunk.

Disturbing the Peace: Any act which disturbs the peace and quiet of others around you.

Divorce: The break up of a marriage.

Docket: The schedule of trials to be heard in a court of law.

Domicile: A place where someone lives.

Donate: To give something. At the time of their death, many people donate their organs to others requiring organ transplants.

Driving While Intoxicated (DWI): Drinking and driving. Also known as Driving Under the Influence (DUI).

Duress: Pressure or forced. If you are forced or coerced into doing something by someone else, for example, then you were acting under duress.

E

Eavesdrop: To listen to the conversation of two or more people without their permission.

Emancipation: To free a parent of any legal duties toward his or her child. This action is usually initiated by the child in an effort to gain more independence. Many child actors, for example, seek emancipation from their parents. This act is sometimes called "divorcing your parents."

Embargo: A restriction preventing businesses from trading with another country. For example, while South Africa was ruled by a racist government, the United States put an embargo on it, forbidding any American company to trade with it.

Embezzlement: To steal money or items from the company where you work.

Encroach: To allow part of your property to enter someone else's. Many people, for example, complain about the roots of trees that are encroaching on their property from their neighbor's yard.

Endorse: Sign your name on the back of a check that has been written to you in order to credit it to your bank account or convert it to cash.

Enjoin: To command or order.

E.P.A.: Environmental Protection Agency.

Equitable: Just and right. To be treated equitably is to be treated fairly.

Escape Clause: Part of a contract that enables one of the parties in the contract not to live up to the duties required by the contract. The escape clause is generally considered a form of protection if a contract that turns out to be unfair in the long run.

Esquire: The title granted to a lawyer.

Estate: The sum total of assets owned by a person.

Estate Tax: The tax levied on items that are bequeathed to relatives through a will.

Euthanasia: Mercy killing. To put someone out of their suffering.

Evict: To kick someone out of a house or apartment that they have been renting. Generally, a landlord must have a good reason to evict a tenant, such as the tenant's failure to pay rent.

Evidence: Anything that supports your argument. In a murder trial, evidence might be a suspect's fingerprints. In a fender bender, evidence might be photos of the damage to your car.

Excise Tax: A tax that is not income tax or property tax.

Execute: To sign something. An executed

document is one which has been signed, indicating that it is an official document.

Executive Order: An order that has come from the President of the United States

Executor: The person named in a will to oversee all matters relating to the will after the time of death.

Executory: Still in progress.

Executrix: The female form of executor.

Exemplars: Evidence that is not the testimony of a witness. For example, photographs of an accident.

Exhaustion of Remedies: Principle stating that no one may begin a court action in the United States without first trying to settle the disagreement outside of the legal system.

Exhibit: A piece of physical evidence.

Exigent Circumstances: An extremely

desperate situation that warrants breaking the law.

Expectancy: The formal term given to real estate indicating that it is not yet possessed by someone, but will be in the near future.

Expend: To spend.

Expert Testimony: Testimony offered at trial by an expert witness. An expert witness is one who has a great deal of knowledge in a particular field, and thus is considered an expert on the subject. In many high profile murder cases, for example, expert witnesses are asked to give their opinions on blood and DNA samples.

Expiate: To attempt to correct a mistake.

Express: Not implied. Stated.

Expropriate: To take.

Expunge: To remove or destroy.

Expungement of Records: When the court

orders that an accused person's criminal record is destroyed. Usually this is done when someone is found not guilty of a criminal offense, and the court wants the person to have an entirely clean record.

Expurgate: To censor.

Extenuating Circumstances: Circumstances that must be taken into account before coming to a decision. These circumstances generally make one's punishment less severe by the court.

Extort: To coerce or force someone into giving you physical property.

Extrajudicial: An event that does not happen within the court.

Eyewitness: Person who actually saw an event occur and can testify to the event in a court of law.

F

Facilitate: To make it easier for someone to commit a crime.

Fact: Something that is generally known to be true.

Failure of Issue: Not having children or offspring.

Fair Market Value: The reasonable value of an item when sold by a well-informed seller to a well-informed buyer.

False Arrest: When the police unlawfully detain or arrest someone.

False Imprisonment: When the police unlawfully put someone in jail.

False Pretenses: To take an item from someone else by misrepresentation.

False Swearing: To swear that something is true when it is not. Perjury is a form of false swearing that takes place within a court of law.

Falsify a Record: To change a written record illegally.

Family Law: Field of law that covers such issues as marriage, divorce, alimony, and adoption.

Family Court: The kind of court which handles family law matters.

Favored Beneficiary: One who receives more through a will than others.

F.B.I.: Federal Bureau of Investigation.

F.C.C.: Federal Communications Commission.

F.D.I.C.: Federal Deposit Insurance Corporation.

Fealty: Loyalty.

Featherbed: To generate work that is not truly necessary in order to make sure that your job position does not become obsolete.

Federal Court: A court of law with jurisdiction over federal trials.

Federal Reserve System: The national association of banks that helps expedite such ordinary banking procedures as depositing money from one bank to another.

Fee: An amount that is owed for the rendering of services.

Fee Simple: To own something outright, with no strings attached.

Felony: A serious crime where the punishment is usually at least one year in jail.

Fence: Someone who conducts transactions of stolen property.

F.H.A.: Federal Housing Authority.

Fiduciary: Someone whose relationship with someone else is based on trust.

Fighting Words: Antagonizing and hostile comments that do not fall under the protection of the First Amendment (the freedom of speech).

Final Judgment: The judgment which completes a court action.

Finders of Facts: People who have the duty to determine the facts surrounding a legal action. These people include the judge and members of the jury.

Findings: The decisions reached by the various finders of facts in a legal action.

Fine: To make someone pay a dollar amount to an authority in order to punish him or her for misconduct.

Firm Offer: An offer which cannot be revoked or rescinded for a prearranged period of time.

First-Degree Murder: Murder which is premeditated and intentional. Premeditated means that past thought was given to committing the act.

Fixture: An object that has been attached to a house or building, and is therefore considered a part of the house or building. For example, fixed cabinets and cabinet drawers should be left inside a house when you sell it.

Force Majeure: A force that is beyond the control of any party of a contract or agreement, thereby altering the requirements of the contract or agreement.

Forcible Entry: To enter a building or house without permission or authority.

Foreclosure: When a bank takes away a house because its owner did not pay his or her mortgage. The bank then generally sells the house in order to get back its money.

Foreman of the Jury: The head person in a jury, who has the added responsibility of acting as the unified voice of the jury when addressing the judge.

Forensic: Relating to the legal system.

Foreseeable: Something that can be reasonably anticipated. For example, in the foreseeable future, you will celebrate your next birthday.

Forfeit: To lose something because you did not live up to the requirements of an obligation. For example, if you do not pay your mortgage, then you forfeit your house to the bank which issued the mortgage.

Forge: To create a false document or written record.

Forum: Any place where a dispute is settled. A court is an example of a forum.

Foundation: Basic evidence introduced into a legal proceeding.

Franchise: A privilege or right granted by the government to an individual or a group.

An example is the right to vote. If someone is disenfranchised, then he or she has a privilege removed.

Franchisee: The recipient of a franchise.

Franchisor: The individual or group granting a franchise. Generally, in legal terms, the franchisor is either a business or the government.

Fratricide: To murder your sibling.

Fraud: An intentional misrepresentation of the truth that is made to someone else in order for personal benefit. For example, if you know your car needs serious repairs, and you sell it to someone by telling them that it runs like new, then you are committing fraud.

Freedom of Assembly: The right for a group to gather together peacefully. This right is granted by the United States Constitution.

Freedom of Expression: The rights to the

freedom of the press, speech, and religion. These rights are granted under the United States Constitution.

Freedom of the Press: The right for any individual or group to publish any item without the interference of the government. This right is part of the freedom of expression.

Freedom of Religion: The right for an individual to practice whichever religion he or she chooses. This right is part of the freedom of expression.

Freedom of Speech: The right to speak your mind on any subject without the interference of the government. This right is part of the freedom of expression.

Fruit of the Poisonous Tree: Evidence that cannot be used in court because it was collected illegally.

Futures Contract: A contract that states that a transaction will occur at a predetermined future date.

G

Gag Order: An order issued by the court that prohibits the parties in a legal matter to discuss their views on the matter with the press.

G.A.O.: General Accounting Office.

Garnishment: When the court orders someone who controls a debtor's money or property to pay a debt on the debtor's behalf.

General Contractor: A licensed individual who does construction or other work to a piece of property that is intended to beautify it or increase its value.

Generation-Skipping Transfer: A transfer of property that skips a generation. For example, if your grandparents were to give you their house, then you would have engaged in a generation-skipping transfer.

Gift: An item that is given to someone else by choice and without the obligation to do so.

Good Faith: Honesty when conducting business.

Goods: Any personal property belonging to an individual, except for his or her house.

Graft: Corruption.

Grandfather Clause: Part of a new law that prevents it from affecting those persons already performing an activity that is regulated by the new law. For example, when the third brake light was added to all cars sold in America a few years ago, owners of cars which had only two brake lights did not have to retroactively install third brake lights.

Grand Larceny: The act of stealing an amount of money (or any items valued at that amount) that is above a certain value. This value differs from state to state. Grand larceny is one of the most serious types of stealing.

Grant: To assign or give something to someone else.

Grantee: The individual receiving the grant.

Grantor: The person giving the grant.

Grantor-Grantee Index: A list generally maintained by a local authority that summarizes all real estate transactions in an area, including the names of the grantors and grantees.

Gratis: Free. Without charge.

Gratuity: A gift.

Gravamen: The main issue of a complaint.

Gross Negligence: To be negligent in performing your duties during a situation where such negligence is likely to harm another.

Gross Profit: Any revenues you receive from an investment or business venture, before subtracting any costs or expenses occurred in attaining the profit.

Ground Rent: Rent paid by the owner of a building on a piece of property to the owner of the piece of property.

Guarantee: An agreement that includes an unconditional promise of certain results.

Guardian: A person who takes care of either a minor under the age of eighteen or another person who is not able to take care of himself or herself.

Guest Statute: A code which limits the amount of responsibility that a driver has to his passengers should an accident occur that is his or her fault.

Guilty: Not innocent. To be convicted of committing a crime.

H

Halfway House: An institution where prison inmates or mental patients serve their sentences that offers more freedom than a true prison or sanitarium.

Hazardous Materials: Items which could cause damage to the environment or harm other people. These items are restricted in their use, and must be handled very carefully.

Hearing: A proceeding where a decision is derived at in light of the evidence presented. A court trial is an example of a proceeding.

Hearsay: Second-hand information. This information is generally not allowed to be used as evidence in a court.

Heir: The person who inherits all or part of a decedent's estate.

Heir Apparent: The person who stands to inherit part or all of a decedent's estate so long as he or she does not die first.

Hereditaments: Any item or part of an estate that can legally be willed to someone.

Hit and Run: To be involved in a car accident and leave without identifying yourself.

Holder: Person who holds a promissory note or I.O.U., and is therefore owed payment.

Holding: An item or asset that is owned.

Holographic Will: A will that is fully executed but does not meet some of the legal technicalities generally required of a will. It is usually up to a court of law to decide whether or not the will should be adhered to.

Homestead: A house and the land it is built on.

Homicide: The slaying of another person.

Hot Pursuit: A high speed chase by police officers of a criminal suspect that often crosses state lines.

Hung Jury: A jury that is not able to decide on a verdict.

Hypothecate: To use an item as collateral on a loan.

I

Illegitimate Child: A child whose parents were not married.

Immigrate: To move to a foreign country and take up residence there.

Immunity: Freedom from liability. One who is immune cannot be held accountable.

Impanel: When a court selects its jurors.

Impeach: To formally accuse a public officer of a crime.

Implied: Not stated. Suggested.

Impost: Tax.

Impound: To take something away from someone and leave it in the custody of the police. For example, if you do not pay your parking violations, the city will impound your car. You will then have to go to the police station and pay any outstanding amounts in order to get your car back.

Improve: To alter a house or building permanently in such a way that it raises that house or building's property value.

Impunity: See immunity.

Inalienable: Not transferrable. Inalienable

rights, for example, cannot be taken away from someone.

In Camera: In chambers. Sometimes, when a judge wants to speak privately with the parties involved in a legal proceeding, he or she will meet them in his or her private office, which is generally referred to as a chamber. In camera refers to any activity taking place within that private office.

Incapacity: Unable to act on one's own behalf. People who are unable to act on their own behalf (i.e., retarded or insane people) are not allowed to sign contracts.

Incarcerate: Send to prison.

Incendiary: Anything causing a fire.

Inchoate: Incomplete.

Income: Moneys earned by working or investing.

Incompetency: See incapacity.

Incorporate: To create a corporation, which is a type of business that has certain characteristics. An example of these characteristics is the fact that individuals who work for the corporation cannot be held accountable for any official action taken by the corporation.

Incriminate: To implicate in a crime.

Indemnify: To insure. When something is insured, the insurance company agrees to assume any responsibilities resulting from that insurance. For example, if you insure yourself against injury or sickness (health insurance), then the insurance company agrees to pay your hospital bills. In order to insure something, a premium must be paid, which is the fee for receiving insurance.

Indemnity: A contract relating to indemnification or insurance.

Independent Contractor: Someone who is contractually obligated to perform a service, but does not have to perform that service in a specific fashion. Whereas an employee must report to work at certain hours, for example, an independent contractor does not.

Indict: To charge with a crime.

Indignity: Mental or emotional cruelty.

Inform: To charge with a crime in writing.

Infraction: A violation of a minor law, where the resulting punishment is the paying of a fine.

Infringe: To use something without authorization.

Inherit: To receive items of property through a will.

Injunction: A court order mandating that something must or must not be done.

In Limine: At the beginning.

Inmate: A convicted criminal serving his sentence in prison.

Innuendo: That part of the complaint in a libel action which sets forth why a particular statement was offensive.

In Perpetuity: Forever.

Inquest: The examination performed on a dead body by a medical official to discover the cause of death.

Insanity: A mental disease which prevents someone from acting according to the normal rules of conduct of society.

Insolvent: Unable to make payment on debts.

Instructions: Directions that a judge gives to a jury during a trial.

Insurance: See indemnify.

Insured: The party who receives insurance.

Insurer: The party giving insurance.

Integration: To put a contract in writing.

Integration usually involves the dismissal of any previous oral agreements that the parties in the contract had prior to writing the contract. Oral agreements are agreements which are made through speech, rather than in writing.

Intent: The reason for doing something.

Interest: Income earned by putting your money into a bank account or a certificate of deposit.

Interlocutory: Temporary. Not permanent.

International Law: The laws which regulate the ways in which different countries interact.

Interplead: When someone with several outstanding debts gives his money and assets to a court of law, with the understanding that the court will then decide the fairest way in which to divide the money and assets between the various entities to whom the debts are owed.

Interrogatories: Written questions.

Intestate: The state of passing away without having a will. A court of law must then assign an administrator to oversee the bequeathing of the items in the estate.

In Toto: In total. In sum.

Invasion of Privacy: To intrude into someone's personal matters.

Inventory: A list of items that are presently in stock.

Invitee: Anyone invited onto a piece of property by an owner or lessee. By definition, an invitee cannot be trespassing so long as the invitation is still in effect. If the invitee is asked to leave but refuses to do so, then he is no longer an invitee.

Involuntary: Unwilling.

Irrelevant: Not pertaining to the issues at hand.

Irreparable Damage: Damage or injury which cannot be repaired. Any moneys paid to the victim of irreparable damage, therefore, must take into account the adverse effects that the irreparable damage has had on the victim's lifestyle.

Issue: An individual portion of a matter that is in dispute. In the case of a fender bender, for example, one issue is the amount of damage caused, and another issue is assigning the blame for causing such damage.

J

J.D.: Juris Doctorate (the law school degree which must be obtained by individuals wishing to practice the law).

Joinder: When two or more different complainants file complaints against a single defendant, and the multiple complainants agree to merge their complaints into one.

Joint Custody: When divorced parents share the rights and responsibilities of taking care of their children.

Joint Tenancy: A piece of property that is owned by more than one person, where all of the owners have equal access to it. One provision of joint tenancy is that if one of the tenants dies, then his percentage of ownership (along with all of its rights and responsibilities) is passed on to the surviving tenants.

Judge: The impartial arbitrator who presides over a trial. The judge is responsible for weighing issues of the law. For example, if a suspect is found guilty of a crime by a jury in a criminal trial, then the judge must decide for how long he or she will go to jail.

Judgment: A judge's final decision.

Judgment Notwithstanding the Verdict: A decision by a judge reversing the decision made by the jury, because the jury's decision is not valid.

Judgment Creditor: Creditor who wins a decision against a debtor. In other words, the debt must be paid.

Judgment Debtor: Debtor who loses a decision to a creditor. The judgment debtor must then pay the debt.

Judgment Lien: Decision allowing a judgment creditor to foreclose the mortgage on a piece of property owned by judgment debtor in order to receive payment for the debt.

Judgment Proof: Someone who is financially unable to pay the damages awarded in a judgment.

Judicial Review: When a decision is turned over to a court with even higher authority through the appeals process. During judicial review, the higher court has the right to support or reverse the decision of the lower court.

Judicial Sale: A decision mandating the sale of an item or asset in order to make payment on a debt or damages.

Judiciary: The legal system.

Jural: Relating to the law.

Jurat: Portion of an affidavit stating the name and title of the official before whom the testimony was sworn.

Jurisdiction: The parameters within which an entity has authority. For example, state courts have authority to hear trials regarding matters of state law, while federal courts have authority to hear trials regarding matters of federal law.

Jurisdictional Amount: Financial parameters regulating a court's jurisdiction over a trial. For example, any trial where an amount of under $5,000 is contested immediately falls into the jurisdiction of small claims court.

Jurisprudence: The study of the law.

Jury: Group of people who make a decision regarding the facts of a case. In criminal cases, for example, the jury decides whether or not the suspect is guilty. There are twelve people in a jury. The jury is not responsible for determining the law surrounding a case once the facts have been determined. The judge must make decisions about the law, and he does so by handing down an appropriately harsh or lenient sentence to someone who has been found guilty.

Jury Trial: Trial which includes a jury in the process of attaining a verdict, or decision.

Justiciable Controversy: A valid dispute which cannot be settled outside of a court of law, and must therefore be settled within a court of law.

Justifiable Homicide: Killing another person in order to defend oneself.

Juvenile Court: Court that hears trials relating to minors under the age of eighteen.

K

Kidnap: To take and detain a person without their consent.

Kin: Relative.

Kleptomaniac: A mental disorder whereby the victim cannot control an urge to steal things.

L

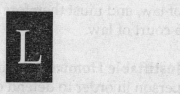

Land Contract: A contract pertaining to the sale of land or property.

Landlord: Someone who owns a building

or house and rents it out to other individuals for a monthly fee.

Lapse: To lose a right or privilege by not fulfilling your obligations. For example, if you do not pay your rent each month, then your lease will lapse, and you can be evicted.

Larceny: Stealing.

Lascivious: Obscene and vulgar.

Last Will and Testament: Full name for a will.

Lawful Entry: The rightful entry of a premises. In order to have the right to enter, you must either possess a warrant issued by a court, be the owner or tenant of a premises, or be the invitee to the premises. Lawful entry is the opposite of unlawful entry.

Lawyer: An attorney.

Lease: Agreement between a landlord and a

tenant in which the landlord rents out a premises to a tenant for a specific period of time and for a specific amount of money to be paid in increments, usually monthly.

Leave of Court: When a judge grants permission for someone in a legal action to do something.

Legacy: An item that is bequeathed in a will.

Legal: Without breaking the law.

Legal Age: Age at which someone is no longer considered a minor, generally eighteen.

Legal Description: An exact description of a piece of property that conforms to standardized guidelines for indicating such information as size, location, and ownership.

Legal Interest: The most expensive rate of interest that a creditor can charge a debtor on a loan without being in violation of usury laws.

Legal Tender: Cash. Coins and bills minted or printed by the appropriate agency for use in purchasing goods and services.

Legal Title: Document indicating ownership of an item or property.

Lessee: A tenant.

Letter of Intent: A preliminary piece of writing indicating that a contract will be written between several parties. The letter of intent specifies the intentions of everyone entering into the contract, without actually going into the specifics of the contract.

Letter Ruling: A letter sent to an individual by the Internal Revenue Service indicating that agency's decision on a tax issue.

Levy: To collect on a debt.

Liable: Having an obligation to someone else.

Libel: Writing something that is made available to the public and that harms someone else's reputation.

License: Permission to participate in an activity, or a document which indicates such permission.

Licensee: An entity or individual who has been granted a license.

Licensor: The entity or individual who grants a license.

Lien: A debt owed on an item or piece of property. The creditor to whom the debt is owed may take and sell the item or property if the debtor does not make payments.

Lineup: A line of suspects organized by the police from which a witness or victim to a crime must pick the person they believe perpetrated the crime.

Liquidate: To sell an asset for cash.

Litigant: One of the parties in a legal matter.

Littoral: Pertaining to seashores, lake shores, or ocean shores.

Locus: Place or location.

Loiter: To linger in one place for no apparent purpose.

Lunacy: Insanity.

M

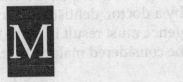

Magistrate: An unbiased arbitrator with less power than a judge.

Maim: To injure someone in such a way that they lose the functions of part of their body.

Majority: Age at which someone is no longer a minor, generally eighteen.

Maker: Person who executes an I.O.U., and is therefore indebted to the holder of the I.O.U.

Malice: Intention to harm someone.

Malicious Prosecution: To involve someone wrongfully in a legal action. It is against the law to sue someone when there is no basis for doing so.

Malpractice: Negligent fulfillment of duties by a doctor, dentist, or lawyer. This negligence must result in harm in order for it to be considered malpractice.

Mandate: An order made by a judge.

Mandatory Injunction: A court order mandating that something be done.

Manslaughter: The killing of an individual that is not premeditated or characterized by malice. Whereas one commits murder if he stalks and kills a woman, he commits manslaughter if he accidentally hits and kills someone with his car.

Maritime Law: The laws pertaining to international commerce and shipping routes. Also known as admiralty law.

Marriage: When a man and a woman are joined together as husband and wife, and this joining is recognized by the state.

Material: Evidence is characterized as material if it pertains to the legal issues in dispute in an action. For example, pictures of the damage to a car caused by a fender bender would be material evidence in the action, but pictures of your house would not.

Material Witness: A witness possessing unique facts pertaining to a legal action. In other words, no other witness in the case knows what this witness knows.

Matricide: The slaying of one's mother.

Maturity: The time at which payment on a debt is due and payable.

Mediation: A form of conflict resolution that is held outside a court of law. The mediator, or arbitrator, is generally trained in the art of compromise, so that both parties will be as happy with the decision as possible.

Mental Cruelty: When one spouse emotionally and mentally abuses the other, without ever resorting to physical violence.

Merger: The joining together of two companies into one.

Meritorious: Worthy and worthwhile.

Metes and Bounds: A standardized fashion by which to describe a piece of land. Metes refers to the lengths of its boundaries, and bounds refers to their directions.

Minor: An individual who is under the age of eighteen.

Minority: A member of a group of people which comprises a smaller number than other groups within the population. African Americans are an example of a minority group in the United States today.

Minutes: Written record of the events and statements made during a trial.

Misappropriate: To use money in a way that is not legal.

Misdemeanor: A crime that is not very serious. Generally, the maximum penalty for a misdemeanor is one year in prison.

Misfeasance: Inappropriate conduct.

Misnomer: An incorrect name.

Misprison of Felony: The act of witnessing a felony and not reporting it to the proper authorities, especially with the intention to conceal the fact that the crime occurred.

Misrepresentation: A lie.

Mistake of Fact: An error associated with a fact utilized in a contract. For example, writing an incorrect date on the contract is a mistake of fact.

Mistake of Law: A conclusion or decision that is in error based on the set of facts given.

Mistrial: A trial that cannot be completed due to either an unforeseeable event, such as the hospitalization of one of the parties, or to a hung jury.

Mitigating Circumstances: Facts associated with a legal action that reduce a party's liability in that action. For example, if a breach of contract occurs, but that breach was accidental, then the punishment will be less severe.

Mitigation of Damages: An attempt to lessen the severity of the damages you have received. If you are involved in a fender bender, for example, and you are aware that continuing to drive your car before you get it fixed will result in even more damage, then you should not drive it until it has been fixed. The person who hit your car is not liable for any damages that you did not attempt to mitigate (i.e., any damages resulting from your continuing to drive the car before it was fixed).

Modus Operandi: Operating method. Fashion in which you work. Criminals tend to have a fixed modus operandi from which they do not vary. For example, someone who breaks into houses by picking locks usually will not break into houses by smashing a window.

Moiety: Half.

Moral Turpitude: With base moral standards.

Mortgage: A loan granted by a bank to an individual in order to buy a house, condominium, or piece of property. The collateral on the loan is the house, condominium, or piece of property itself. Generally, monthly payments are required on the part of the debtor in order not to be in default of the loan.

Mortgagee: The debtor when a loan is specifically a mortgage.

Mortgagor: The creditor when a loan is specifically a mortgage.

Motion: A request made to a court regarding an issue of law. As such, the decision on a motion is made by a judge, not the jury.

Movant: Party initiating a motion.

Move: To make a motion.

Mulct: A fine.

Municipal Court: A court where the jurisdictional amount is generally under $25,000.

Murder: The slaying of a person that is characterized by premeditation and malice.

N

Naturalization: The act of becoming a citizen of a foreign country.

Naturalized Citizen: Someone who is a citizen of a country through the naturalization process.

Natural Person: An individual. An artificial person is an entity that, for the purposes of the law, is treated like an individual. A company is an example of an artificial person.

Necessity: A defendant in an action can claim that he acted out of necessity if his actions were in order to save himself or others from harm or death.

Negligence: The failure to fulfill a required duty or obligation with due care. This failure must directly result in harm being caused to a person in order for it to be considered negligence.

Net Profit: The total profit after any costs and expenses incurred have been subtracted from the gross profit.

Next Friend: An individual who takes the place of a minor during a legal action, but is not that child's parent or legal guardian.

Next of Kin: The closest surviving relative.

No Contest: In a criminal case, the suspect is always asked whether he pleads guilty or not guilty to the charge. If he pleads no contest, he is pleading neither guilty nor not guilty.

Nominal: Minor and relatively insignificant.

Non-Competition Agreement: An agreement which limits someone from competing with someone else. If, for example, you work at an ice cream store where they make homemade ice cream, and you are asked to sign a non-competition agreement, you cannot go to work for another ice cream store or open your own store and make the same homemade ice cream. The reason for this is that you learned everything you know from your employer, and it would be unfair to use that knowledge competitively against it.

Nonconforming Use: A use for land that does not comply with current zoning laws that is permitted because the land was adopted for that use prior to the enactment of the current zoning laws.

Nonfeasance: Failing to do something.

Nonrecourse: Having no personal liability. For example, many mortgages have a nonrecourse clause, indicating that if the debtor does not pay his mortgage, the lender can take the house, but he cannot sue the debtor.

Non Sui Juris: Incompetent.

Non-Support: Not providing child support or alimony, in direct disobeyance of a court order.

No Strike Clause: A clause included in many contracts between companies and their employees that prevents the employees from striking as a means of voicing their complaints.

Notary Public: A lesser official who has the authority to administer such oaths as affidavits.

Note: An I.O.U.

Not Guilty: Innocent. To be acquitted of committing a crime.

Notice: A written statement sent out to all

parties involved in a legal action informing them of any developments in the action. It is illegal not to send a notice when one is required.

Novate: To release one or more of the original parties from a contract and to replace them with new parties. This action can only be done with the agreement of every party to the contract.

Nugatory: Not valid.

Nuisance: To prevent someone else from enjoying his own property by pestering or bothering him. If enough people are bothered by the act of nuisance, then it becomes an act of public nuisance, which annoys many members of the community.

Null and Void: Not valid.

Nullity: Something that is not valid.

Nuncupative Will: A will that is recited orally. Such wills are very difficult to prove valid in a court of law, and should be avoided at all costs.

O

Oath: To swear an oath is to swear to the truth of a statement or testimony.

Objection: A challenge to a statement made or a question asked by opposing counsel in court. A lawyer essentially objects to the actions of his opponent if he feels those actions are unfair, irrelevant, or are trying to confuse the issues.

Obloquy: State of very ill repute.

Obscenity: Anything which appeals to the prurient interests, that is below the moral standards of the community at large, and lacks any serious purpose. Proving that something is obscene (such as a pornographic movie) is one of the most difficult things to do in a court of law, as different people have such varying interpretations of what obscenity means. One famous judge could give no better a definition of obscenity than, "I know what's obscene when I see it!"

Obstruction of Justice: Preventing the legal process from being served. For example, if you prevent a police officer from arresting a suspect, then you can be charged with obstruction of justice.

Occupancy: The state of living in a building or house.

Occupational Disease: An illness that directly results from your work. For example, many construction workers who labor with asbestos get cancer.

Odium: With hatred and malice.

Offense: An act of breaking the law.

Ombudsman: A lesser official who receives complaints from individuals directed toward the government, and tries to resolve these complaints through mediation.

Omission: Failing to do something.

Open Court: A court trial where the general public is allowed to attend and watch the proceedings.

Opening Statement: At the beginning of a trial the attorneys for the plaintiff and for the defendant each make opening statements to the jury and judge. These statements essentially summarize their arguments, and hint at the kind of evidence that is going to be presented in support of that argument.

Open Shop: A business where the employees are not required to become members of a union.

Operating Expenses: The costs and expenses associated with running a business or engaging in an activity. Such expenses must be deducted from gross profits in order to calculate net profits.

Opinion: A written record in which the judge issues his decision and his reasons for reaching this decision.

Opprobrium: Without honor.

Option: A right secured by contract to buy an item at a specific price before a specific date. The option does not require the item to be bought, however, and the contract is simply nullified if it is not bought for the right right price before the deadline passes.

Order: A decision made by a judge about one of the lesser points of a legal action, but not a final judgment. The order almost always requires that one of the parties in the action perform some duty, such as paying a fine to the opposing party.

Ordinance: A local law.

Ouster: To illegally kick out the rightful owner of a premises.

Overreaching: Using coercion or fraud as a means of making someone else conform to your will.

Overrule: When a lawyer makes an objection in court, the judge can either overrule or sustain the objection. To overrule the objection means that the judge does not consider the objection to be valid.

Overt: Made public, not hidden.

P

Pactum: Agreement.

Pain and Suffering: Damages awarded by the court in order to help alleviate any mental and physical pain and suffering that has been caused to a victim.

Palimony: A form of alimony that is paid when a couple breaks up that has never been legally married, but has lived together for so long that they are essentially married.

Paralegal: An assistant to a lawyer who conducts legal research and helps draft legal documents.

Pardon: To excuse a person from punishment after they have been convicted of committing a crime.

Parole: The shortening of a prison sentence as long as the criminal does not break any other laws. Parole is generally offered to prison inmates as a reward for good behavior.

Partnership: When two or more individuals start a business together and have all of the rights and responsibilities of co-owners of that business. The co-owners must share all of the profits from the business, as well as all of its operating expenses.

Party: An individual or entity who is either the plaintiff or defendant in a legal action.

Patent: An acknowledgement by the government that an individual or entity has invented or discovered something. That individual or entity has the sole right to profit from the invention or discovery for a fixed amount of time from the issuance of the patent.

Paternity Suit: A type of legal action that seeks to prove that a man is the father of a baby. This type of suit is generally used as a means of requiring the father to make child support payments.

Peculate: To embezzle.

Pecuniary: Relating to finances or money.

Penal Code: The set of laws which are concerned with criminal offenses, such as murder or robbery. These codes also indicate guidelines for the kind of punishments that judges can assign to convicted criminals.

Per Annum: Per year.

Peremptory: Conclusive and final.

Perjury: To lie while under oath to tell the truth in a court of law.

Permissive Waste: Waste that results from someone's failing to do something. For example, if the roof of your apartment leaks, then you must contact the landlord and arrange to have it fixed. The landlord must pay for these repairs. But if you do not call him for several weeks, and allow the carpet to get ruined, then you are responsible for the cost of repairing the carpet, as these wasteful repairs are the result of your failing to call promptly.

Personal Property: All items owned by a person other than real estate. Also known as personalty.

Petition: A request made in writing.

Petitioner: Anyone making a petition.

Petty Offense: See misdemeanor.

Pilfer: To steal. Usually, pilfering refers to stealing small items and trinkets.

Plagiarize: To use someone else's words as if they were your own. For example, college students must cite all references when they write a term paper, or they are plagiarizing the source from which they received a piece of information.

Plaintiff: The complainant in a legal action. The person who sues the defendant.

Plead: When a suspect responds to the judge's query of innocence or guilt.

Plenary: Complete and entire.

Polygamy: To be married to more than one spouse at a time.

Possession: To have an item under your control. For example, if your car is parked in your garage, and you have the keys to it, then it is in your possession. If you loan it to someone else, you still own it, but it is out of your possession.

Power of Attorney: The assigned power to act on someone else's behalf.

Precedent: The results of a previous legal action which is similar to a current action, precedents give the judge of the current action a basis from which to make his decisions.

Prejudice: Bias.

Premeditation: Planning in advance.

Prenuptial Agreement: A contract between a husband and wife that specifies how their joint estate will be divided up if they get a divorce. The contract is executed before the marriage commences.

Pretermitted Heir: An heir born after a will has been executed. If the will is not changed prior to the death of the decedent, then a court hearing is usually required to determine how much of the estate will be bequeathed to the pretermitted heir.

Probate: Proving the validity of a will.

Pro Bono: For the good. Pro Bono legal services are performed free of charge, as they are considered to be for the common good.

Promissory Note: I.O.U.

Proprietor: Owner.

Prosecution: The equivalent of the plaintiff in a criminal trial. The party that initiates a criminal action by accusing a suspect of committing a crime.

Prosecutor: The lawyer who is on the side of the prosecution.

Proximate Cause: The cause of an injury.

Proxy: Someone who acts on someone else's behalf.

Public Domain: Information that is not copyrighted. For example, 18th century classical music is now so old that it is in the public domain and can be played by anyone without the permission of the composer's descendants.

Puff: To give an opinion.

Punishment: A penalty assessed on someone who has broken a rule.

Punitive Damages: A form of financial punishment. For example, if someone who runs a red light in their car hits you, causing you to go to the hospital with injuries, then the judge might order the driver of the car to pay your medical bills. The judge might also order the driver to pay punitive damages, an amount of money so great that it acts as a form of punishment for failing to stop at the red light.

Purview: Purpose.

Putative: Alleged.

Q

No entries

R

Racketeer: To commit extortion.

Ratable: Able to be taxed.

Real Property: Real estate. Any piece of land, including any buildings, houses, or other structures built upon it.

Realty: Another word for real property.

Rebut: To counter or disprove.

Recant: To take back a statement.

Reciprocity: Agreements that extend between state and national borders. For example, Canada and America have reciprocity agreements. Thus, if you are an American tourist in Canada and get a parking ticket, then your United States Department of Motor Vehicles record will reflect that ticket.

Reckless: Without care.

Record: A document in writing which sets forth an occurrence or event. For example, a receipt is a record of a sale.

Recoup: To recover from a loss by gaining money.

Redress: Remedy.

Rely: To trust or count on someone.

Relinquish: To give up.

Remand: To send to a lesser authority. For example, if you sue someone in Superior Court, but the amount you are suing for is less than $25,000, then the Superior Court judge will remand your case to a lower court, such as Municipal Court (the jurisdiction of Superior Court generally includes money values of over $25,000).

Remedy: Damages paid to someone suffering from an injury.

Rent: A fee paid for the right to occupy property. Generally, rent is paid on a monthly basis.

Reparation: See remedy.

Repeal: To take back.

Repossess: To seize the collateral for a loan when a creditor is unable to make payments. For example, if you have to make monthly payments on your car, but you are unable to do so, then you could have your car repossessed.

Represent: To act as an attorney on someone's behalf.

Rescind: To make a contract null and void.

Residence: A place to live in.

Resident Alien: Someone who lives and works in one country while maintaining citizenship status of another country.

Residue: The remainder of a decedent's estate after everything he or she bequeathed to relatives has been given away.

Retainer: The down payment that a client makes to his or her lawyer when the lawyer agrees to take the case.

Retract: To take back.

Revenue: Any financial income.

Revoke: To take back an offer.

Rider: See addendum.

Rob: To steal something. Robbery is distinguished from burglary in that the victim must be present during a robbery, and the victim must face possible harm from the robber. In other words, if you come home one night and find all of your belongings taken, then you have been burgled. If, on the other hand, someone sneaks into your house with a gun and steals all of your possessions, then you have been robbed.

S

Sanction: A financial punishment or fine.

Satisfy: To make payment on a debt.

Scienter: Knowledge that a false testimony has been given.

Search Warrant: A court order allowing a police officer or other official to enter a private location, such as an office or home.

Securities: Investments in a business.

Security Deposit: Down payment that a tenant makes when renting or leasing an apartment, house, office, or retail space. If the tenant fails to pay his or her rent, or if the tenant leaves the apartment or house damaged at the end of the lease, then the owner has the right to deduct the appropriate costs from the security deposit.

Sentence: A punishment that is handed down by a judge.

Sequester: To keep a jury together during the course of a trial, so that they can reach conclusions without being affected by the viewpoints of other people not related to the legal action.

Service of Process: To officially deliver a legal document to the opposing party in a legal action.

Silent Partner: A partner in a business who invests money and receives a share of the profits, but who does not perform an actual function in the running of the business.

Slander: To harm another by verbally making comments that could affect his reputation negatively.

Small Claims Court: The lowest level of courts in the American legal system, small claims courts cases cannot exceed a disputed amount of $5,000.

Sole Proprietor: Someone who owns and operates his own business.

Solicitor: The name for a lawyer in England.

Standing: The right to sue someone or engage in a legal proceeding. In order to have standing, one must have been harmed in some way.

Statute of Limitations: The deadline before which a legal proceeding must be started. Different types of proceedings have different deadlines. For example, some serious crimes have a deadline of up to 25 years, whereas less serious offenses might have a deadline of only a year. One cannot seek justice after the statute of limitations has expired.

Stay: An official postponement by the court.

Stipulate: To agree in writing. A stipulation is usually part of a larger agreement, such as a contract.

Sublet: When a tenant rents out the property in which he resides to someone else with the agreement of the owner.

Subpoena: A written document demanding an appearance in court during a legal action. To ignore a subpoena is a very serious crime.

Suicide: To kill oneself.

Suit: A legal action.

Summons: A legal document issued to a defendant indicating that a lawsuit is being filed in court. The defendant has a certain amount of time to respond to the summons in an appropriate fashion, or else the plaintiff wins the action by default.

Superior Court: The state court with the highest jurisdiction, hearing cases too big for either municipal court or small claims court.

Suppress: To prevent something from happening.

Surrogate: Someone who performs an action for someone else. Thanks to medical science, for example, surrogate mothers now exist.

Suspended Sentence: When a convicted party's punishment is waived, even though it is recognized that he was found guilty of committing a crime.

Sustain: To agree with or approve.

T

Tacit: Suggested.

Tamper: To change something without permission to do so.

Tangible Personal Property: Items that you own other than money or real estate, i.e. cars, jewlery, silverware, etc.

Tariff: A tax.

Tax: An obligation owed to someone with authority. For example, anyone who works in this country has the responsibility to pay income tax to the government, in return for which the government provides benefits to its citizens, such as paving highways.

Tenant: Someone who resides in a home, apartment, office, or retail space with the permission of the owner. The tenant must pay a rent to the owner in exchange for this, generally on a monthly basis.

Tenancy in Common: This type of joint ownership allows one owner to sell his share or put it in his will without the consent of the other owner or owners.

Tender: To offer.

Term: The times of the year when a court is open to hearing cases. Just as with school, there are certain times during the year when some courts shut down.

Testify: To give statement while under oath not to lie.

Testimony: The statements made by one who testifies.

Title: A document indicating the ownership of a piece of land or other property.

Tort: A kind of matter handled in civil courts that does not involve contracts. For example, if you have a contract with someone to fix your car, and he fails to do so, then you are involved in a breach of contract dispute. If, on the other hand, you get into a fender bender (where there is no contract between you and the other driver), then you are involved in a tort dispute.

Tort: Any private or civil wrong (other than breach of contract) that results in an injury to a person or property.

Transcript: A written record indicating the events and statements made during a proceeding. For example, transcripts are written for every legal action that takes place in a court of law in this country.

Treaty: A type of agreement between countries.

Trespass: To enter onto someone else's property without their permission.

Trial: A legal action that is supervised by a judge.

Trust: A fund that is intended for someone but is held out of their possession until they reach a certain age or agree to use the moneys in the fund for a certain purpose. For example, with the rising cost of a college education, many parents start saving for a college trust fund when their children are born.

Trustee: The person or institution that manages and oversees a trust.

U

Ultimate Facts: The facts in dispute during a legal action. These facts must be proved or disproved through evidence.

Unclean Hands: Guilty of wrong-doing.

Unlawful Entry: To enter onto someone else's property through some form of misrepresentation. For example, if a police officer claims to have a writ allowing him to enter your house, but he does not actually possess one, then he is guilty of unlawful entry.

Usury: To charge an exorbitant rate of interest on a loan. There are strict laws governing the highest rates that may be charged by lenders.

V

Vacate: To leave. For example, if you do not pay your rent, then your landlord has the right to ask you to vacate the premises.

Vandal: Someone who destroys or damages public or private property.

Vend: To sell.

Vendor: Seller.

Vendee: Buyer.

Venire: A list of jurors, or the type of writ used to summon those jurors to appear in court.

Venue: The appropriate place for a trial to be held. In determining the correct venue for a trial, a lawyer must take into account the jurisdictions of the different kinds of courts in this country, and then choose the appropriate one. In some cases the lawyer mistakenly chooses the wrong venue, in which case the trial is then remanded to the appropriate court.

Verdict: The conclusions reached by a jury. As the jury must determine the facts surrounding a legal proceeding, a jury verdict can only be either guilty (the facts as presented by the plaintiff are correct) or not guilty (the facts as presented by the plaintiff are incorrect).

Verification: A special kind of affidavit that attests to the truth of a statement.

Void: Nullified. Not in effect.

Voir Dire: Speak truthfully.

W

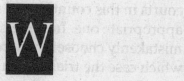

Waive: To give up a right to something.

Wanton: Reckless.

Ward: Someone who requires the guardianship of another. For example, a child is the ward of its parents.

Warrant: A court order allowing police officers to enter a specific building or arrest someone.

Warranty: A promise or guarantee.

Wedlock: Marriage.

White Collar Crime: Crimes that do not involve violence.

Waiver of Immunity: Allows a witness to give up his or her right to refuse to testify against himself or herself. This makes it possible for the person's testimony to be used against them.

Will: The written record of how a decedent wants his or her estate divided up. Wills are frequently contested in court, so they must be written in strict accordance to federal and state laws. Lawyers who deal with wills are called probate lawyers.

Willful: With intent.

Witness: Someone who expresses a fact during a legal proceeding. The expression of fact is called a testimony.

Workers' Compensation: Benefits paid to an employee who suffers a work-related illness or injury.

Writ: A written court order that demands a specific action to be completed by a specific time.

X

No entries.

Y

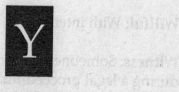

Yield: The rate at which profits are returned on an investment. For example, if you put some money in a bank account, and you make 6% interest on that money, then your yield is 6%.

Z

Zoning: Laws governing the way land can be used in certain areas. For example, you cannot build a skyscraper in a suburban residential community.

Conclusion

Now that you have had a chance to look up some of the words that you might have found troublesome in the past, I just wanted to leave you with a few parting thoughts.

First, as you can now see, most of this terminology is not that difficult to understand. It may be complex, but that does not mean it is difficult per se. You see, the nature of the American legal system is such that details are excruciatingly important. Manslaughter and murder, for example, are two forms of killing, but their slight differences make a huge legal distinction. Therefore, the distinction between the two words naturally makes them more complex, but the definition of each word is not difficult to understand.

Second, you have to understand that being an attorney is being a member of a trade. If you belong to a trade yourself, then you are aware that all trades naturally generate their own terminology and jargon. If you're a carpenter, then you must use words like "shim" and "joist" all the time, but most people have no idea what these words mean; likewise, if you are an electrician, then you probably use such mysterious terms as "watts," "ohms," and "grounded." Why do different trades allow their own distinct sets of vocabulary to evolve? This is difficult to say. Some people suggest that by having a unique vocabulary, a trade gains credibility and mystery; the members of that trade know some information that you do not.

At any rate, the most important thing to remember is that complicated words are still merely words. If there is a term that you don't understand, then you can simply look it up. If you're still having trouble, then why not take a trip down to a nearby law school, and pay a visit to the law library. Any of the librarians there would be happy to assist you. They have years of experience under their belts. So you see, there is no reason for you not to understand any legal term you ever come across. It might take you some time and effort to discover its definition, but there is nothing secret or magical about it that prevents you from learning its meaning.

I hope that you have gained a great deal of knowledge from reading the *Legal Reference Library*. I certainly learned a great deal from writing it. I am sure that all three volumes will be useful for me for years to come (which is the real reason why I wrote it!), and I hope that they have the same value for you.

I also want to remind you that you have done what very few people have the confidence to do: you have taken it upon yourself to learn more about the legal system. Most people view the legal system as a huge beast that is far beyond their control, so they are scared silly about the whole thing. But not you. You have demonstrated the courage to tackle a challenging subject, and you are now a bigger person for it.

Congratulations! I hope that your future is free from legal troubles.

Notes

Notes

Notes

Notes

Notes